For K-12 SCHOOL HARMONICA BAND and HOME STUDY

MEL BAY PRESENTS

Youth Harmonica Method

David Barrett's Complete Harmonica Masterclass Lesson Series   *By David Barrett*

> Thanks to Dennis Carelli and Stu Yager for editing and proof reading. Thanks to Mrs. Dorothy Martin on Piano. Also, to my wife Nozomi and our family for their never-ending support.

Learn to read music, play popular songs, and be part of an ensemble! For the C Major Diatonic Harmonica

CD contents

#	Track	#	Track	#	Track
1	A Word from the Author	25	Happy Birthday	49	We're Tenting Tonight
2	Chording & Rhythm	26	Ding Dong Bell	50	Home on the Range
3	Chording & Rhythm	27	Home Sweet Home	51	Silent Night
4	Chording & Rhythm	28	Red River Valley	52	Blues Band
5	Chording & Rhythm	29	What of Christmas	53	*Bonus Track*
6	C Note	30	Sixteenth Run	54	Lovely May (Piano)
7	C & D Walk	31	Riding Sixteenths	55	Fox and Goose (Piano)
8	Walk & Rest	32	Hold On	56	Twinkle, Twinkle, Little Star (Piano)
9	Climbing	33	Triplet Walk	57	Baa! Baa! Black Sheep (Piano)
10	Climbing Faster	34	Row, Row, Row Your Boat	58	This Old Man (Piano)
11	Blow Bounce	35	Oh, Susanna!	59	Are You Sleeping (Piano)
12	Draw Bounce	36	Jingle Bells	60	Blow the Man Down (Piano)
13	Elevator	37	Entire Harmonica Pitch Set	61	She'll Be Comin' Around the Mountain (Piano)
14	No! No! No!	38	Big Swing		
15	Lovely May	39	Swing Train	62	Happy Birthday (Piano)
16	Fox and Goose	40	Comin' and Goin'	63	Ding Dong Bell (Piano)
17	Twinkle, Twinkle, Little Star	41	Horn Man	64	Home Sweet Home (Piano)
18	Baa! Baa! Black Sheep	42	The Royal Coachman	65	Red River Valley (Piano)
19	C & D March	43	Home Sweet Home	66	What of Christmas (Piano)
20	Eighth Note Climb	44	Good Night Ladies	67	Row, Row, Row Your Boat (Piano)
21	This Old Man	45	Amazing Grace	68	Oh, Susanna! (Piano)
22	Are You Sleeping	46	Old Black Joe	69	Jingle Bells (Piano)
23	Blow the Man Down	47	America	70	Comin' and Goin' (Piano)
24	She'll Be Comin' Around the Mountain	48	Old Folks at Home	71	Horn Man (Piano)

1 2 3 4 5 6 7 8 9 0

© 2005 BY MEL BAY PUBLICATIONS, INC., PACIFIC, MO 63069.
ALL RIGHTS RESERVED. INTERNATIONAL COPYRIGHT SECURED. B.M.I. MADE AND PRINTED IN U.S.A.
No part of this publication may be reproduced in whole or in part, or stored in a retrieval system, or transmitted in any form or by any means, electronic, mechanical, photocopy, recording, or otherwise, without written permission of the publisher.

Visit us on the Web at www.melbay.com — E-mail us at email@melbay.com

Contents

A Word from the Author – Track 1 3
Material Needed 3
Placing Your Lips on the Harmonica 4
Holding the Harmonica 4
Chording & Rhythm – Tracks 2-5 5
Note Reading & Rhythm Training 6
Solo Harmonica Songs 7
    C Note – Track 6 7
    C & D Walk – Track 7 8
    Walk & Rest – Track 8 8
    Climbing – Track 9 8
    Climbing Faster – Track 10 8
    Blow Bounce – Track 11 8
    Draw Bounce – Track 12 8
    Elevator – Track 13 9
    No! No! No! – Track 14 9
    Lovely May – Track 15 (Piano Track 54) 9
    Fox and Goose – Track 16 (Piano Track 55) 9
    Twinkle, Twinkle, Little Star – Track 17 (Piano Track 56) 10
    Baa! Baa! Black Sheep – Track 18 (Piano Track 57) 10
    C & D March – Track 19 11
    Eighth Note Climb – Track 20 11
    This Old Man – Track 21 (Piano Track 58) 11
    Are You Sleeping – Track 22 (Piano Track 59) 11
    Blow the Man Down – Track 23 (Piano Track 60) 12
    She'll Be Comin' Around the Mountain – Track 24 (Piano Track 61) 12
    Happy Birthday – Track 25 (Piano Track 62) 13
    Ding Dong Bell – Track 26 (Piano Track 63) 13
    Home Sweet Home – Track 27 (Piano Track 64) 13
    Red River Valley – Track 28 (Piano Track 65) 13
    What of Christmas – Track 29 (Piano Track 66) 14
    Sixteenth Run – Track 30 14
    Riding Sixteenths – Track 31 14
    Hold On – Track 32 15
    Triplet Walk – Track 33 15
    Row, Row, Row Your Boat – Track 34 (Piano Track 67) 15
    Oh, Susanna! – Track 35 (Piano Track 68) 15
    Jingle Bells – Track 36 (Piano Track 69) 16
Entire Harmonica Pitch Set – Track 37 16
Solo Blues Harmonica Songs 16
    Big Swing – Track 38 17
    Swing Train – Track 39 17
    Comin' and Goin' – Track 40 (Band Track 70) 17
    Horn Man – Track 41 (Band Track 71) 17
Harmonica Band 18
    The Royal Coachman – Track 42 18
    Home Sweet Home – Track 43 20
    Good Night Ladies – Track 44 23
    Amazing Grace – Track 45 25
    Old Black Joe – Track 46 27
    America – Track 47 30
    Old Folks at Home – Track 48 32
    We're Tenting Tonight – Track 49 34
    Home on the Range – Track 50 36
    Silent Night – Track 51 39
    Blues Band – Track 52 41

A Word from the Author

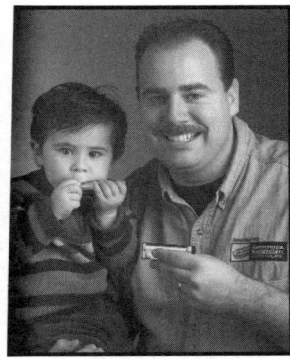

Welcome to *Harmonica Masterclass'® Complete Harmonica Lesson Series*. My name is David Barrett, and I'm the author of this lesson series. Harmonica is a wonderful instrument that offers people of all ages the chance to express themselves through music. To play an instrument well takes hard work and perseverance. With good study habits and a genuine desire to learn how to play, you will do just fine. After you have completed this book, refer to the back cover for details about the entire *Harmonica Masterclass Lesson Series*. If you have any questions regarding this book, or any other books within the line, look at the Harmonica Masterclass website at www.harmonicamasterclass.com, or contact us by mail at PO Box 1723, Morgan Hill, CA 95038. Good luck and have fun!

Material Needed

Harmonica You will need a C major ten-hole diatonic harmonica for this book and recording. For the Harmonica Band songs you will need a Hohner 365C harmonica if you choose to play the bass parts.

CD Player Whether you are studying this course by yourself at home or with a harmonica band at school, the CD included with this book will be very helpful to make sure your notes are correct and your rhythm is strong. For easy CD navigation, the example numbers in black boxes are also the track numbers on your CD.

Placing Your Lips on the Harmonica

The **Tilted Embouchure** is achieved by opening your mouth as pictured left. Place the harmonica in your mouth with the front of the harmonica tilted downward as pictured right. With slight pressure, press the harmonica into your bottom lip. If you hear a little bit of either adjacent hole, tilt the harmonica more, or bring the sides of your lips in a bit.

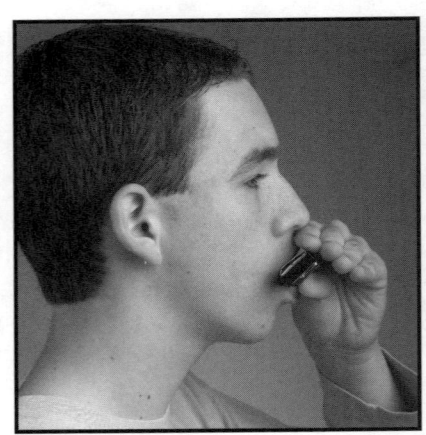

Holding the Harmonica

The first rule of holding the harmonica is to not cover your playing surface. Notice in the pictures above that the upper lip covers a large area of the top cover plate. Make sure that your fingers do not get In the way of your lip placement.

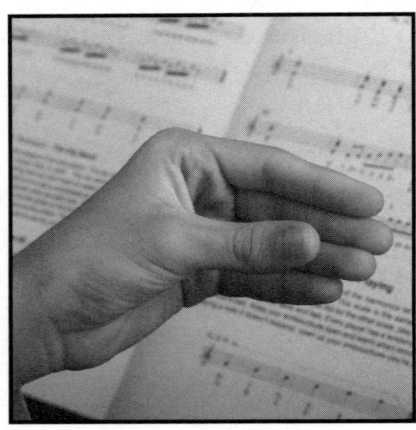

Pictured left is how your left hand should look before placing the harmonica in your hand. Pictured right shows how the harmonica sits in that cradle. The harmonica might fall out at this point. Therefore, we need the other hand and your lips to help seat the harmonica. Pictured below and to the left shows where your right hand is placed.

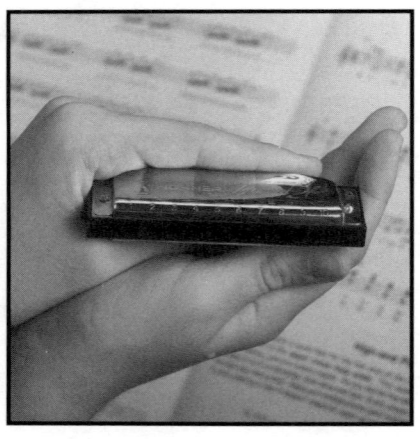

Do not close the back of your cupped hands; we want the sound to go to the listener. Pictured at right is how the back of your hands are open and relaxed. If you want to practice quietly, you can close the back of your hands to cup in the sound. The tighter you cup, the less sound that comes out.

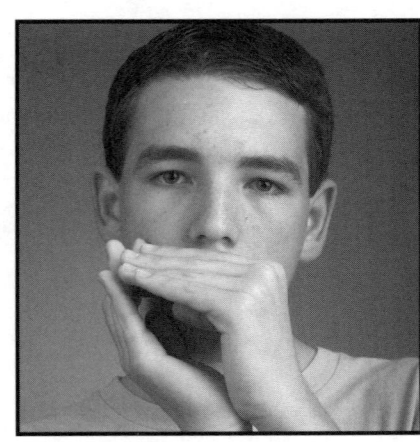

Chording & Rhythm

Before we start playing songs, let us spend some time working on breathing through the harmonica in rhythm. We will use the word **Blow** when exhaling through the harmonica and the word **Draw** when inhaling through the harmonica. When blowing or drawing, always keep the air passage through your nose closed; we want all air going through the harmonica.

2 Start counting by saying "1 2 3 4 1 2 3 4 1 2 3 4 etc." all the numbers should be spaced evenly within time. As you count, tap your foot to each number. Every set of four (1 2 3 4) equals one *Measure*.

3 Start tapping your foot in time. Place your lips over the first through fourth holes and draw for one measure (four beats), and blow for one measure. Repeat this in time, counting in your head. Don't blow or draw too hard, think soft and warm.

| 1 2 3 4 | 1 2 3 4 | 1 2 3 4 | 1 2 3 4 | 1 2 3 4 | 1 2 3 4 | 1 2 3 4 | 1 2 3 4 |
Draw------ Blow------ Draw------ Blow------ Draw------ Blow------ Draw------ Blow------

Now do the same for two measures (two sets of four beats).

| 1 2 3 4 | 1 2 3 4 | 1 2 3 4 | 1 2 3 4 | 1 2 3 4 | 1 2 3 4 | 1 2 3 4 | 1 2 3 4 |
Draw-------------------- Blow-------------------- Draw-------------------- Blow--------------------

And now for three measures (three sets of four beats). If you cannot play this long, maybe your nose is open.

| 1 2 3 4 | 1 2 3 4 | 1 2 3 4 | 1 2 3 4 | 1 2 3 4 | 1 2 3 4 |
Draw--------------------------------- Blow---------------------------------

And finally for four measures (four sets of four beats). Most students will not be able to play four measures this early in their playing. Do not worry if you cannot play for this long, it will come with time and practice.

| 1 2 3 4 | 1 2 3 4 | 1 2 3 4 | 1 2 3 4 | 1 2 3 4 | 1 2 3 4 | 1 2 3 4 | 1 2 3 4 |
Draw-- Blow--

4 With the same lip placement on the harmonica, let us now try using **HA** to help each note stand out. For each beat (tap of the foot) say HA. Draw for one measure and blow for one measure, and repeat. Now try the same using **TA**. Make sure when saying the "A" part of the syllable that your jaw and tongue drops (like when you yawn).

| 1 2 3 4 | 1 2 3 4 | | 1 2 3 4 | 1 2 3 4 |
Draw------------ Blow---------------   Draw------------ Blow---------------
HA HA HA HA HA HA HA HA   TA TA TA TA TA TA TA TA

5 Let us now take the same passage and swing it. When your foot is down, that is called the **Downbeat**. When your foot is up, it is called the **Upbeat**. The downbeat is counted with a number and the upbeat is counted with an "and" (&). Resist the urge to tap your foot down for the number and the "and." You can use either the HA or TA articulation.

```
| 1 & 2 & 3 & 4 & | 1 & 2 & 3 & 4 & |
Draw--------------------------- Blow---------------------------
TA TA TA TA TA TA TA TA  or  HA HA HA HA HA HA HA HA
```

Note Reading & Rhythm Training

Staff: The music staff has five lines. Time moves from left to right on the staff.

Ledger Lines: The lower lines hold notes that are low in pitch. The upper lines hold notes that are high in pitch. Sometimes notes go beyond the five lines and ledger lines are used to help keep your place.

Treble Clef: The treble clef symbol is placed at the beginning of a staff to give a reference pitch. You can see that the bottom curl encircles the second line from the bottom. This second line is the pitch G. Because of this, the treble clef is also known as the *G Clef.*

Notes on the Line: Notes are found on each line of the staff and ledger lines. The notes **E G B D F** found on the staff can be remembered by using "**E**very **G**ood **B**oy **D**oes **F**ine."

Notes in the Spaces: Notes are also found in the spaces. The notes **F A C E** found on the staff can be remembered by using "**FACE**."

Stem Direction: Notes are placed on these lines and spaces that tell you how long to hold a note. You will see notes that have stems. Some stems point upward and some stems point downward. Stem direction does not change the pitch or length of a note.

Time Signature, Bar Line & Ending: The line that dissects the staff is called a ***Bar Line***. The time between two bar lines is called a ***Measure***. The thin bar line and thick bar line at the end of the staff tells you that the song is over. The ***Time Signature*** is placed at the beginning of a piece of music to tell you how many beats are in a measure and which note duration is to receive the beat. The 4/4 time signature shows that there are four beats per measure and the quarter note receives the beat.

Note Durations: A whole note is held for a count of four beats, or one whole measure. A half note is held for a count of two beats, or half a measure. A quarter note is held for one beat, or one quarter of a measure.

Pitch & Duration on the Staff: This example shows: the 4/4 time signature; a C whole note for the first measure; a C half note and A half note for the second measure; and B, A, G, and F quarter notes for the third measure.

Solo Harmonica Songs

7

17 Twinkle, Twinkle, Little Star

New Rhythm
Dotted Half Note

A dot to the right of a note extends its value by half. The half note receives two beats. The dot is half of its value, one beat. This makes the dotted half note receive three beats.

18 Baa! Baa! Black Sheep

New Rhythm
Eighth Note & Rest

The eighth note receives one half a beat. When two eighth notes are used next to each other, one will start on the downbeat (when the foot is on the ground) and the other will start on the upbeat (when your foot is in the air). The eighth note uses one flag. If two eighth notes are used next to each other, their flags are beamed together.

19 C & D March

20 Eighth Note Climb

21 This Old Man

New Note & Pickup Measure

In the next song there are only two beats (two quarter notes) at the start. This is called a *Pickup Measure*. When counting off the next song, the C starts on the third beat. When there is a pickup measure, the last measure will also have the same amount of beats as the first.

22 Are You Sleeping

New Time Signatures & Notes

3/4 Three Beats per Measure
Quarter Note Receives the Beat

2/4 Two Beats per Measure
Quarter Note Receives the Beat

23 Blow the Man Down

24 She'll Be Comin' Around the Mountain

25 **Happy Birthday**

Fermata (Hold note until conductor moves on.)

New Rhythm
Dotted Quarter Note & Rest

The quarter note receives one beat. The dot is half of its value, one half a beat. This makes the dotted half note receive one and one half beats. The dotted quarter note is usually followed by an eighth note.

26 **Ding Dong Bell**

27 **Home Sweet Home**

28 **Red River Valley**

13

29 What of Christmas

New Notes & Rhythms
Sixteenth Note & Rest

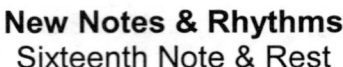

Dotted Eighth Note & Rest

Triplet Notes

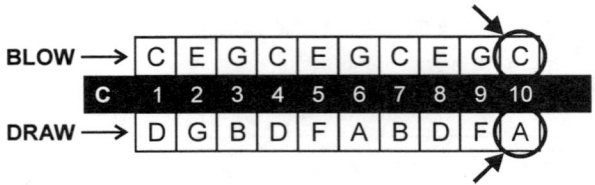

The sixteenth note receives one quarter of a beat. The sixteenth note is often found after a dotted eighth note. The eighth note receives one half a beat. The dot is half of its value, one quarter of a beat. This makes the dotted eighth note receive three quarters of a beat. The triplet eighth note receives one third of a beat. The triplet will most commonly be seen beamed in a group of three. This group of three takes up one beat.

30 Sixteenth Run

1 e & a 2 e & a 3 e & a 4 e & a   1 & a 2 & a 3   4

31 Riding Sixteenths

14

36 Jingle Bells

Entire Harmonica Pitch Set

Shown below are all of the notes available on your ten hole major diatonic harmonica. Hole numbers have been placed below the notes for reference. A hole number standing by itself is to be drawn and a hole number with a plus is to be blown.

37

Solo Blues Harmonica Songs

When playing blues harmonica you will use much more of the lower range of the harmonica. When reading music on the staff, the lower four holes go very low into the ledger lines. For the upcoming blues songs we will transpose the notes one octave higher so that they are on the staff. This will make the G on the staff a six blow. Blues rhythms also use swing eighth notes. Listen to the recording for an example of swing eighths.

38 **Big Swing**

Repeat Bar (Repeat from beginning.)

39 **Swing Train**

40 **Comin' and Goin'**

41 **Horn Man**

17

Harmonica Band

Many different size classes can play the following harmonica band arrangements. If there are ten students in the class, place two students per part and double the melody (top line) with four students. If it is just you and a friend, one can play the top melody line and the other can play the bottom bass line. The bass part is played using a Hohner 365 C diatonic harmonica. The bass part can also be played with a Hohner 280C chromatic harmonica.

42 **The Royal Coachman**

19

43 Home Sweet Home

44 **Good Night Ladies**

24

45 Amazing Grace

46 Old Black Joe

47 America

48 Old Folks at Home

49 We're Tenting Tonight

35

50 Home on the Range

51 Silent Night

6/8 Time (Six beats per measure, eighth note receives the beat.)

52 Blues Band

As in the previous blues songs, you will play all the parts one octave lower and swing the rhythms.

45

Practice Record

Week	Assignment & Amount of Hours Practiced Per Day							Parent's Initials
	Monday	Tuesday	Wednesday	Thursday	Friday	Saturday	Sunday	
1								
2								
3								
4								
5								
6								
7								
8								
9								
10								
11								
12								
13								
14								
15								
16								
17								
18								
19								
20								
21								
22								
23								
24								
25								
26								
27								
28								
29								
30								
31								
32								
33								
34								
35								
36								